Polluted
Planet

Jen Green

Chrysalis Children's Books

First published in the UK in 2004 by
Chrysalis Children's Books
An imprint of Chrysalis Books Group plc
The Chrysalis Building, Bramley Road,
London W10 6SP

ISBN 1 84458 067 9

British Library Cataloguing in Publication Data for this
book is available from the British Library.

Editorial Manager: Joyce Bentley

Produced by
Tall Tree Ltd
Designer: Ed Simkins
Editor: Kate Simkins
Consultant: Michael Rand
Picture Researcher: Lorna Ainger

Printed in China

Some of the more unfamiliar words used in this book
are explained in the glossary on page 31.

The Publishers would like to thank the following for their
kind permission to reproduce the photographs:

Alamy: Bill Bachmann 26, front cover tr
Robert Battersby/Tografox 9b, front cover tl
Corbis: Brian Bailey 27t, Chinch Gryniewicz/Ecoscene
2, 14, back cover, Nick Hawkes; Ecoscene 13t,
Pavlovsky Jacques/Sygma 19t, front cover br, Le
Segretain Pascal/Sygma 7t, Joseph Sohm;
ChromoSohm Inc. 15b
Hulton Getty 7b
PA Photos: EPA 16, 19b, 24, Haydn West 25b

Still Pictures: 27b, Martin Bond 5t, 31, MarkEdwards
12, 22, 29, M. Farmer/UNEP 17b, Peter Frischmuth 6,
front cover c, 21b, Dylan Garcia 13b, Paul Glendell 4,
30, Russell Gordon 5b, Reinhard Janke 20, Brigitte
Marcon 8, Andre Maslennikov 10, front cover bl,
Jean-Francois Mutzig 15t, Ray Pfortner 11,
J.Rajab/UNEP 1, 17t, Hartmut Schwarzbach 23t,
Jorgen Schytte 23b, Roland Seitre 25t, Andrew Testa
18, David Woodfall 21t

Contents

What is pollution?

For millions of years, life has existed on Earth, because the planet provides all the conditions needed for living things. Now, however, people are damaging nature by producing harmful waste called pollution.

There are many different kinds of pollution, from dirty smoke and spilled oil to untidy litter. Farms, factories, homes and cars all produce pollution, as they give off waste products called pollutants. Pollution has got worse recently as the population and the number of factories have increased.

▼ *Pollution sometimes happens because of accidents, such as oil spills. In 1996, the tanker* Sea Empress *struck a rock off the Welsh coast and spilled oil that damaged local beaches.*

Pollution spreads on the wind and through soil and water. It is now found all over the world, even in faraway places, such as Antarctica, where there are no factories.
In recent years, we have discovered a lot more about the damage pollution is causing. Many people are now working to tackle pollution, and everyone can help.

◀ *Some pollution happens deliberately, such as when people carelessly drop litter.*

LOOK CLOSER

Some kinds of pollution have natural causes. For example, erupting volcanoes give off clouds of ash and poisonous gas that harm the atmosphere. However, volcanoes only erupt from time to time. Most pollution caused by humans, such as car fumes and smoke from factories, occurs all the time.

Air pollution

Earth's atmosphere is made of a mixture of gases, including nitrogen, oxygen and carbon dioxide. Clean air is vital to living things. Polluted air harms people and wildlife.

Industry is one of the main sources of air pollution. Factories and power stations give off poisonous gases as they burn fossil fuels – coal, oil and gas – to produce energy. Cars, trains, ships and planes also release pollutants as they burn fuel.

▼ The tall, narrow chimneys of this power station in Germany are releasing pollution. Steam billows from the wider funnels of the cooling towers.

In cities, the air is getting more polluted because of cars, factories and power stations. When heated by sunlight, some of the polluting gases produce a dirty, poisonous haze called smog. Smog damages plants and causes breathing problems. Many countries are now trying to reduce the pollution that is causing smog.

▲ Smog is now a problem in major cities all over the world. This cyclist is wearing a protective mask.

CLOSE TO HOME

Smog is not a new problem. In the 1950s, smog caused by sooty smoke from coal fires in homes and factories killed over 4000 people in London. The British government had to pass laws to reduce smoke given off by homes and factories.

Hidden dangers

As well as harming people and wildlife, air pollution causes other problems. For example, it is causing Earth's climate to get warmer – a danger called global warming.

For millions of years, gases in the air, such as carbon dioxide, have helped to warm the planet. They have the same effect as the glass in a greenhouse, and so are called greenhouse gases. Factories, homes, cars and power stations are now adding more greenhouse gases, which is trapping too much heat. In future, global warming looks likely to bring flooding as the seas warm up and expand.

▼ *Global warming is starting to melt the ice in the polar regions. The more the ice melts the more sea levels will rise, which may cause coastal areas to flood.*

UV rays from the Sun

Ozone layer

Hole in the ozone layer

Earth

A layer of ozone gas high in the air helps to screen us from harmful rays in sunlight. However, pollution has recently damaged this layer. Gases called chlorofluorocarbons (CFCs), used in fridges, spray cans and foam packaging, attack ozone. This has caused ozone holes to appear above the polar regions. Many countries have now agreed to stop using these gases, but the damage will still last for years.

CLOSE TO HOME

Ultraviolet (UV) radiation from sunlight causes illnesses, such as skin cancer, in humans and animals. Damage to the ozone layer means that it is especially important to wear suntan cream and protective clothing whenever you spend time in the Sun.

Acid rain

Some types of pollution spread from the air to soil or water. One example is acid rain, which harms living things and even eats away at stone or rock.

Acid rain is caused by waste gases that are given off by cars, power stations and factories. When these mix with water vapour in the air, they form a weak acid. This then falls as acid rain. The acid damages the leaves of trees and plants. Many thousands of trees in Europe and North America are now affected by this problem.

▶ Acid rain has killed these trees in a forest in Poland. In Germany, the problem is called Waldsterben, which means "forest death".

LOOK CLOSER

The waste chemicals given off by cars and factories include sulphur dioxide and nitrogen oxide. These react with water and sunlight to form sulphuric acid and nitric acid. The acid rain falls to Earth, polluting rivers and lakes and killing trees.

Factories produce waste gases

Acid rain falls from clouds

Chemicals react with water vapour in clouds

Rain water pollutes lakes

Acid rain drains into soil

Acid rain kills trees

Acid rain drains into the ground, where it harms tiny living things, including fungi and bacteria. These fungi and bacteria help to break down dead plants and animals to fertilise the soil, so acid rain means that the soil becomes less fertile. The acid also upsets the chemical balance of lakes. This harms fish, such as salmon, and other water creatures.

▶ *Acid rain has eaten away at this stone statue in New York City, USA, spoiling the carving.*

Water pollution

Plants, animals and other living things need clean water to survive, yet the oceans and many rivers and lakes are now affected by pollution, mainly caused by the dumping of waste.

▼ *In poorer parts of the world, many rivers are tainted by sewage. Using dirty water for drinking, washing or cooking can make people ill.*

Around the world, many rivers and lakes are polluted. Factories on riverbanks tip chemicals into the water. In some areas, sewage from homes is pumped into rivers. When farmers on nearby land spray chemicals on their crops, some drain off the land and into the water. Much of this pollution is carried downstream to the sea.

For centuries, the oceans have been used as a giant dustbin for all kinds of waste. People used to think the seas were so vast it would have no effect, but this isn't so. Seaside ports and factories pump chemicals into the shallows, while some kinds of very poisonous waste are dumped far out at sea. Water pollution is spread by waves, tides and currents. Once in the sea, it is almost impossible to remove.

Rivers can become more polluted as they flow from high ground to the lowlands. Check your local river or pond for signs of pollution, such as foam, litter, smelly or coloured water, or dead fish and birds.

◄ *This barrel containing dangerous waste was dumped far out to sea, but tides and currents carried it back to land.*

Land pollution

Pollution can harm the ground under our feet as well as the air and oceans. Pollution spreads more slowly through the soil than through air or water.

The land is most often polluted by the waste we throw away. Every day, homes, shops, offices and factories produce huge quantities of rubbish. Most of this gets buried in pits called landfills. Poisonous chemicals sometimes leak from these sites into water under the ground. This polluted water seeps into rivers and lakes.

◀ *Landfills can be smelly and attract pests, such as gulls and rats, that can spread disease*

◀ *Nuclear waste is stored at this underground site in France. No one has found a way of getting rid of radioactive material, which remains dangerous for thousands of years.*

Mining companies digging for valuable minerals leave huge piles of waste rock around the mine. This pollutes the soil. It also looks ugly. Radioactive waste from nuclear power stations is often buried underground. Great care is taken to avoid leaks from the burial sites, but they sometimes happen.

LOOK CLOSER

In the 1970s, oil containing poisonous chemicals was sprayed on dirt roads to keep down the dust near the town of Times Beach in Missouri, USA. People began to suffer from chest pains and bad headaches. Experts decided that the pollution was so bad that everyone had to leave, and the whole town was sealed off.

Pollution after war

Wars and weapons can have a devastating effect on the environment. In the last 50 years or so, new types of weapons have been developed that are more destructive than ever.

Ordinary weapons, such as explosive shells, can flatten whole streets and damage landscapes. Tanks and troops moving across the land can harm fragile places, such as deserts. This happened during the 2003 war in Iraq.

◄ This memorial in the city of Hiroshima in Japan reminds people of the devastation caused when a nuclear bomb was dropped on the city in 1945. The radiation released 60 years ago still causes serious health problems for the people living there.

◀ *In wartime, pollution is sometimes caused by sabotage – deliberate acts of destruction. During the Gulf War in 1991, these oil wells were deliberately set alight, which caused dangerous chemicals to be released into the air.*

Nuclear and chemical weapons are an even greater threat to the natural world. In 1945, US forces dropped two nuclear bombs on cities in Japan. This caused massive destruction, killing hundreds of thousands of people. In the 1960s, the United States sprayed poisonous chemicals that destroyed forests in Vietnam, Asia, that protected enemy soldiers. The poison devastated the countryside and badly affected people's health.

LOOK CLOSER

The testing of nuclear weapons causes great harm to the environment and to people's health. In the 1950s and 60s, nuclear tests released dangerous amounts of radiation across much of the northern half of the world. This crater in the Nevada Desert, USA, is the site of a nuclear bomb test.

Accidental damage

Pollution sometimes happens because of accidents. Fires in factories, oil spills and even carelessness have caused pollution on a grand scale.

Nuclear power stations have many safety features to prevent dangerous radiation escaping. Even so, accidents have happened. In 1986, a nuclear power station at Chernobyl in the Ukraine exploded after fire broke out. A cloud of radiation polluted northern Europe and beyond. Many people, animals and plants were poisoned, and the effects will last for hundreds of years.

▲ These children were made ill by the radiation from Chernobyl.

▲ Fire fighters inspect the damage after the fire at the Sandoz chemical factory in Switzerland.

In 1986, the River Rhine in western Europe was polluted after fire broke out at a chemicals factory in Switzerland. Poisonous waste killed all life in the river for 100 km downstream. Oil spills at sea and on land have also caused great damage. In 1994, leaks from an oil pipeline near Usinsk in Arctic Russia polluted three major rivers, killing thousands of fish and birds.

LOOK CLOSER

In 1984, an explosion at the Union Carbide chemicals factory in Bhopal, India, released a cloud of poisonous gas. Over 3000 people died, and thousands more were injured. Here a survivor places a candle in front of pictures of some of the victims.

Noise, light and heat

Loud noise and bright lights are kinds of pollution that can be annoying and even dangerous. Heat pollution affects many rivers near factories and power stations.

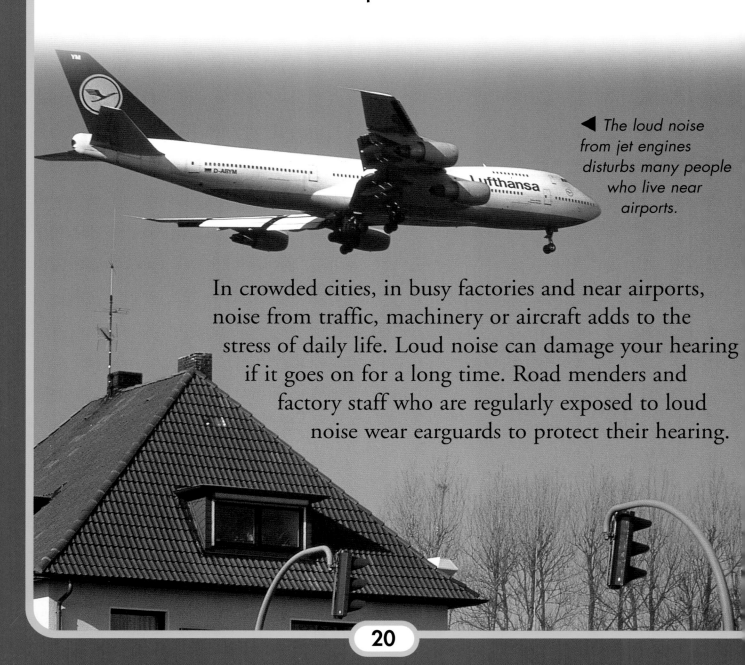

◀ The loud noise from jet engines disturbs many people who live near airports.

In crowded cities, in busy factories and near airports, noise from traffic, machinery or aircraft adds to the stress of daily life. Loud noise can damage your hearing if it goes on for a long time. Road menders and factory staff who are regularly exposed to loud noise wear earguards to protect their hearing.

Factories and power stations often use river water to cool their machinery. The used water they return to the river is warmer than the water they took out. Warm water holds less oxygen than cold water. This harms fish and other water creatures and may stop them breeding. This type of pollution is called thermal pollution.

▲ *A steelworks in Spain empties warmed water back into the local river. Thermal pollution can raise the temperature of rivers and lakes by up to 20°C.*

LOOK CLOSER

In many parts of the world, city lights now brighten the night sky and hide the stars. This can confuse night-active animals who think the lights mean it is daytime.

Cleaning up

Air pollution is harming nature in many ways. All over the world, governments, scientists and ordinary people are now working to clean up air pollution.

Air pollution is being tackled in two different ways. People are cleaning up the damage that has already been done. At the same time, scientists are searching for ways to reduce future pollution. Air pollution is mainly caused by burning fossil fuels. However, not all countries produce the same amount of pollution. Today, rich countries produce more pollution than poor countries, because they have more factories and cars.

▼ *A helicopter drops lime on a lake polluted by acid rain to neutralise the acid. This clean-up technique is expensive and has to be repeated every few years.*

◀ *A child on a busy street is breathing in car fumes. However, these fumes are less dangerous than they once were due to catalytic converters and cleaner fuels.*

Many countries have now passed laws to reduce pollution. Factories and power stations can be fitted with filters that reduce waste gases. Devices called catalytic converters reduce the poisonous fumes given off by cars and trucks.

LOOK CLOSER

Pollution caused by burning fossil fuels can be reduced by using other forms of energy. The Sun's heat and energy from winds and rushing rivers can be used to generate electricity. Unlike fossil fuels, these forms of energy are also "renewable", which means they won't run out.

Tackling pollution

Around the world, people are taking steps to clean up water and land pollution. Governments, individuals and groups that protect nature all play a part.

In recent years, many people have realised the dangers of pollution, thanks to the work of protest groups, such as Greenpeace. These organisations fight to save the oceans and land from pollution. Many countries now have anti-pollution laws that make their seas, rivers and land cleaner and safer for both people and wildlife.

▼ *In August 2002, up to 10 000 people marched to protest about environmental issues outside the UN Earth Summit in Johannesburg.*

One way to tackle the damage done by pollution is to set up reserves or parks, where pollution is limited as much as possible. Antarctica is one such nature reserve.

CLOSE TO HOME

Find out more about pollution and help with the clean-up work by joining an environmental group, such as Friends of the Earth or Greenpeace. You'll find their contact details on page 29.

Since the 1990s, representatives from many countries have met several times and have agreed on measures to tackle pollution. However, some countries, such as the United States, are reluctant to sign the agreements, because they believe it will harm their industries.

How can we help?

Each and every one of us produces some pollution as we go about our daily lives. We can all help to reduce pollution. If everyone does a little, the situation will improve.

All the rubbish we throw away each week adds to the problem of waste disposal. Taking used bottles, tins, plastic and paper to recycling centres helps to reduce both waste and pollution. Litter also causes pollution. Don't drop it!

▼ *Glass, drinks cans, plastic, newspapers, cardboard and rags can all be recycled. Take old clothes, books and toys to charity shops.*

The used water leaving our homes contains strong, harmful chemicals, such as washing-up liquid, soap powder and bleach. These can harm wildlife in local rivers. Cut down on pollution by using "environmentally friendly" cleaning products.

Every day, we all add to air pollution as we use energy made by burning fossil fuels – especially when we travel by car. Everyone can help to cut pollution by using cars less and bikes or public transport more.

▲ Help reduce noise pollution by using earphones with personal stereos. Think of the people around you if you use a mobile phone in a public place.

◄ Cycling to school helps to reduce pollution in your neighbourhood.

Pollution projects

How clean is your neighbourhood? Find out by doing a pollution survey. Try using sand and gravel to filter water as in a water treatment plant.

1. To test for air pollution, you'll need three jar lids smeared with petroleum jelly. On a dry day, place one lid outside your house, another on a busy street nearby and the last in an open space, such as a park. Go back later and see how much dirt has collected in each lid.

POLLUTION SURVEY

Wherever you find people, you'll also find pollution. However, some places are a lot more polluted than others. Try these tests to investigate local pollution.

2. Think about noise in your three test areas. Give each marks out of ten. Are different kinds of noise, for example, traffic and machinery, a problem?

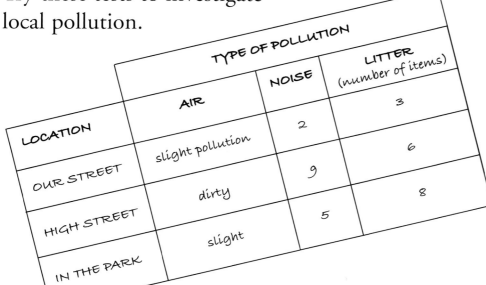

LOCATION	TYPE OF POLLUTION		
	AIR	NOISE	LITTER (number of items)
OUR STREET	slight pollution	2	3
HIGH STREET	dirty	9	6
IN THE PARK	slight	5	8

3. Litter is another form of pollution. Check each site for litter. (Pick it up as you go, but always wear gloves.) Now make a chart, such as the one shown here, to record your results.

MAKE A WATER FILTER

Many water treatment plants filter local water using sand and gravel to make it safe to drink. Try this experiment to see how the technique works. You'll need two clean jam jars, a funnel, coffee filter papers, a little clean sand or gravel, and soil.

1. Stand the funnel in a jar and line it with filter paper. Mix soil and water in the other jar, then pour the mixture through the funnel. How much dirt is removed?

2. Try using a new filter paper with a handful of sand or gravel at the bottom.

3. Now use both sand and gravel as filters. Which filter works best?

Warning: Don't drink the filtered water, as it's still not very clean.

▲ *Examples of filtered water at the different stages at a water treatment plant.*

CAMPAIGN GROUPS

WWF
Panda House, Weyside Park
Godalming, Surrey GU7 1XR
Website: www.wwf.org.uk

Friends of the Earth
26–28 Underwood Street
London N1 7JQ
Website: www.foe.co.uk

Greenpeace
Canonbury Villas, London N1 2PN
Website: www.greenpeace.org

POLLUTION WEBSITES

US Environment Protection Agency: www.epa.gov/globalwarming/kids
also: www.epa.gov/students
and: www.epa.gov/owow/nps/kids
Environmental Investigation Agency: www.eia-international.org
www.kidsagainstpollution.org/
New Scientist Planet Science page: www.newscientist.com
www.worldalmanacforkids.com/explore/environment5.html
www.oneworld.net/penguin/pollution/pollution_home.html
Wastewatch UK: www.wastewatch.org.uk
Recycling: www.kidsrecycle.org

Pollution factfile

• Famous buildings in many parts of the world are now showing signs of acid-rain damage. They include an ancient temple called the Parthenon in Athens, Greece.

• In Britain, experts estimate that around £200 million is spent each year on just keeping machines, such as TVs and computers, on standby. Switching such machines off when they're not being used saves both money and energy.

• In 1979, a disaster similar to the one at Chernobyl, known as a "meltdown", almost happened at a nuclear power station called Three Mile Island in the United States.

• The banning of CFCs, which damage the ozone layer, is an example of how countries can work together to reduce pollution. In 1987, nations worldwide agreed to stop using these dangerous gases by the year 2000, and this has now happened.

• The United Arab Emirates releases more carbon dioxide per person than any other country, followed by the United States.

• The United States holds the record for producing more waste materials per person than any other country. Next comes Australia, then Canada.

Glossary

Acid rain
Rain that is acidic, because it is polluted by waste gases in the air.

Environment
The surroundings in which we live.

Environmentally friendly
Something that does not harm the natural world.

Fossil fuels
Fuels, such as coal, oil and natural gas, that are made of fossilised plants or animals that lived millions of years ago.

Global warming
Warming weather worldwide, caused by the increase of gases in the air that trap the Sun's heat on Earth.

Greenhouse gases
The layer of gases in the air that traps the Sun's heat. Carbon dioxide and methane are greenhouse gases. Too much greenhouse gas causes global warming.

Landfill
A pit in the ground where rubbish is buried. Most of the world's rubbish is disposed of in this way.

Ozone layer
A layer of ozone gas found high in the air, which helps prevent harmful ultraviolet rays in sunlight from reaching the surface of Earth.

Pollutant
A substance that dirties the air, water or land when released.

Pollution
Any harmful substance that damages the environment. Pollution is mainly caused by waste products that people don't want and release into the natural world.

Radioactive
A radioactive material gives off dangerous rays known as radiation.

Recycling
The process of reclaiming useful materials from waste so that they can be used again.

Sewage
Dirty water from homes and factories, containing chemicals and human waste.

Smog
A poisonous, dirty haze that forms in the air when polluting gases react with sunlight.

Thermal pollution
A type of pollution that occurs when warm water is pumped into rivers and lakes.

Index